تطوّر في التطريز

Advances in Embroidery:

Poems, with Translations from Mahmoud Darwish

Ahmad Al-Ashqar

¶oets & traitors press

Traduttore, traditore.

Poets & Traitors Press publishes books of poetry and translations by a single author/translator. P&TP emerged from the Poet/Translator Reading Series and from the New School's Literary Translation Workshop, both of which draw on writers who continue to travel between creative writing and translation, artists for whom one language cannot be enough and whose own utterance carries, shapes, and is shaped by another's.

Poets & Traitors acknowledges support from Stephanie Browner, Melissa Friedling, Raúl Rubio, Alex Draifinger, Jane McNamara, Eugene Lang College, the Bachelor's Program for Adults and Transfer Students, and the New School Foreign Languages Department.

ISBN 978-0-9990737-0-4

Advances in Embroidery: Poems, with Translations from Mahmoud Darwish

The Sandwich Series #1
New York City

SANDWICH SERIES NO. 1

ADVANCES IN EMBROIDERY: POEMS, WITH TRANSLATIONS FROM MAHMOUD DARWISH

AHMAD AL-ASHQAR

table of contents

PREFACE

Sandwiched between two sections of my own poems, the reader will find my translations of Mahmoud Darwish. I hoped to bridge between my experience as a Palestinian poet of the diaspora and that of one who had been inspired by the land, written about the land, and lived on the land itself, which I have not. I hoped this bridge could lead me home.

Darwish is known for his sharp political commentary as it relates to Arab nationalism and the Israeli-Palestinian conflict, and is often enshrined as a symbol of the Palestinian struggle, a child of the *nakba* and *naksa*—a reminder that pain can still be beautiful. And while there is no denying these features are significant throughout his work, in my translations I found it essential that he—being human before Palestinian—also be recognized, even immortalized, for more than nationalism, resistance, and other symbols typically associated with Palestinian identity. Is there not more substance to being an Arab, a Palestinian, a person, than conflict and pain?

I set out to examine Darwish's library of images and motifs to translate not the aggression but the energy of his work. I spent time living in his wordplay and figurative language, losing myself and my own poet's voice in his cadence. In my translations and in many of my own poems here, I wanted to engage with Darwish in a dialogue to underscore his universal themes—all of it through the lens of our shared identity, borne of another's voice yet in my own, present in the grey overlap that plants itself within the fibers of our blood-related styles.

Ahmad Al-Ashqar
Dubai, 2017

advances in embroidery

تطوّر في التطريز

This is for my wife, my son. This is for *Ummi wa Abi*. This is for every child and every woman killed in war. This is for Peace. This is a bridge.

هَلْ غَادَرَ الشُّعَرَاءُ مِنْ مُتَـرَدَّمِ   أَمْ هَل عَرَفتَ الدَّارَ بعْدَ تَوَهمُّ

Have the poets left any garment unpatched?
Or did you find *Home* after hallucinating?

— *Antara ibn Shaddād*

القسم الأول

section 1

MEDITATION ON TEN TOPICS

1. on death

draped in toxic garbs of black,
breathe a final hideous breath,
return as a single strand from
haystack, ask: *how windy, death?*

2. on symbolism

i want to be like them who shred
poetry outside academic spaces
to reveal decay or our proneness
to wasting energies – in this i see
myself older, bearded, enraged.

3. on imperialism

i have watched for years a nation
i call *home* demolishing homes in
my *home. fighting terror* or fighting
fire with firepower & fighter-jets.

4. on identity

today i'm palestinian as i was yesterday,
am tomorrow. face-wrapped you sling
lightning bolts, i am you. trace my lineage in your eyes and ages in your voice.

5. on translation

i have occupied another's voice for
so long i forgot mine; his birds, his
olive-trees, & his longing for home.
i have repeated his repeating lines
in hopes his hilly landscape (which
is also mine) would guide me back.
i have repeated his repeating lines
& found my home in his imagery.

6. on fragrance

my favorite scent: *oud ispahan*
smells like chaos inside a field
of persian roses inside a forest.
i may ask to be embalmed in it.

7. on public transit

all of us in some way or another
have found our face in another's
stinking armpit. & all of us will
at some point before we leave or
die here face an unzipped zipper
or be duly informed of our own.

8. on bullshit

if i've learned anything from
not reading & pretending to
care for film it's that hip-and
-wit *art types* are mad gullible.

9. on courage

my son now maneuvers from the
couch to table to toys, oftentimes
stumbles falling back. oftentimes
when i stumble & fall back i quit
but he always – *always* – gets up!

10. on life

i remember distinctly the feeling that
night in the hospital, my wife in pain
(to say the least) pulsing with a force
i never thought possible – hours later
she birthed a fleshy, crying metaphor.

MEDITATION ON STRUCTURES

1. on brutalism

poured concrete more concrete
more violence more force. more
constants more structures post-
modern war torn. you're ugly &
blocky you're hard at your core.
poured concrete more concrete
make concrete your home.

to create architecture is to put
in order. to put what in order?
to put function and objects.

brutalism stems from *béton-brut*,
french for *raw concrete:* primary
material. repeating modular
elements / repeating modular
elements / repeating modular
elements which form masses
represent functional zones &
group into a complete whole.

surfaces of cast concrete reveal
a basic nature of construction;
concrete is used for cold & raw
unpretentious honesty — thus
concrete is: honest and natural.

dissatisfied with modernist forms
in the mid-1950s the movement
opposed the impractical abstract
& sleek decorations; it was often
associated with socialist utopian
ideology; it was pragmatic, tacit.

in its ruggedness & lack of concern
to look comfortable/calm, brutalism
can be seen as a reaction by younger
architects to the lightness & frivolity
of earlier designers – brutal, honest.

characterized by bold geometries,
exposure of structural materials,
and functional spatial design: an
expression of social progressivism.

characterized by cold symmetry,
exposed, stripped down to core
with hulking & repeating rotes:
expression of post-industrialism.

le corbusier says: a house
is a machine for living in.

brutalism was idealistic, human:
public housing, academic spaces
where honest natural machines–
or humans–convene in *machines*–
or buildings–for tactic functions.

my alma mater, designed by walter netsch
to tell a single brutalist story, was a prison
projecting an atmospheric totalitarianism.

it was vulgar, geometric; but true to itself.
i am vulgar, symmetric; but true to myself.
it was practical, ruthless; but true to itself.
i am modest, impractical; true to myself.

2. on islamic architecture

handassa mu'amariyah islamiyyah is built upon
the mosque, the tomb, the palace, the fort.
tall minarets and curved domes   converge
like prayer-goers at night;   press shoulder-
to-shoulder   hulking across the landscape.

horseshoe arches also known as moorish
arches are derived from spanish visigoths
and curve dramatically, and appear often.

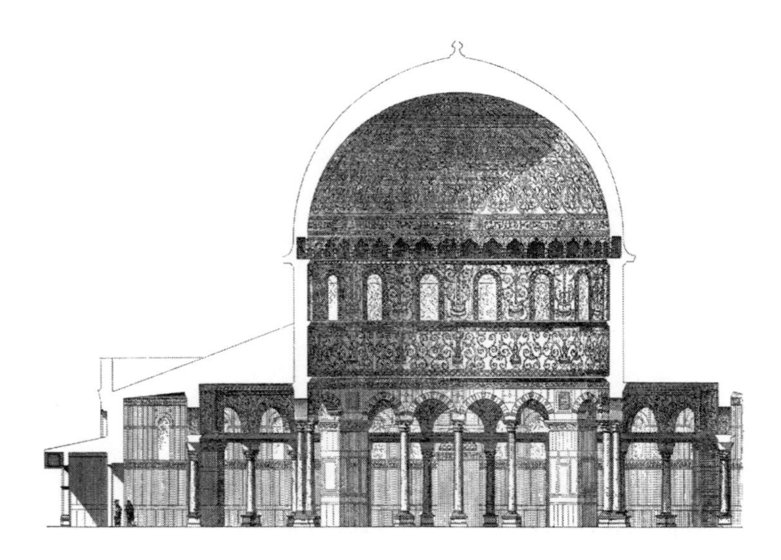

it is: persian, ottoman, byzantine;
fluid in structure;   hallways, wide;
courtyards, grand; and at its core,
communality. technicolor mosaics
with inlaid marble patterns adorn
carvings across walls, halls, floors.

ceramic tiles and later brickwork
stretch from córdoba to xinjiang.

a *sehan*, or courtyard, highlights
architectural elements, provides
shade; often a semi-open arcade.

intra- and inter-cultural hierarchy
of styles suggests wider-reaching
influence, expansion; geometrical
shapes in design and spatial plans
harken to elements of euclidean
lines or, more fittingly, algebraic
cyphers: a congruence, similarity.

intricate stonework on monuments
like those of ancient mesopotamia,
grand and somber, project skyward
looming over villages; the women
in black, silk scarves, men in tunics
gather and chat around a fountain.

DATE-BEARING PHOENIX

i am my own palm tree   shouting down
dates wrinkled and sweet   am my own
leaves rustling filling night with sounds
ominous   my crown's fond an awning
shading travelers   although restless my
cadence it gales through tents removing
paper off tables figured from my trunk

rooted i declare freedom defend terrain
cleanse habitats with my breaths   naked
i stand calm veiled in thick film of sand
i present secrecy   nomad build a shelter
from my stems   i am pillars my strength
in height   bedouin trust your camel tied
to my aching mast   mary shake me my
branch it contains sustenance   summer
sun father wind i am yours: embrace me

CHICKPEAS GARNISHED

with parsley   warm   doused in olive
oil float dominant   in shallow bowls
beside   white ceramic plates of fried
eggs & pickled eggplants. fermented
sour yogurt of the caucasus balances
chili paste. hot sweetened tea in pots
teeming with leaves & stems of sage

– all mediums linking *palette* with *palate*:
one the spread of color before me, the
other in my mouth waiting like crowds
gather at exhibit openings to consume.

mezze, as turks call it, predates canvas;
a collaborative art   in which mothers
& fathers like warhol & basquiat zip
in tempo through kitchens producing
fingerfoods small & even smaller, for
harsh critics: children, kindred, guests.

today and in only underwear my wife
creates alone   impersonating picasso.

> most saturday mornings – the studio a living room,
> the plates a canvas, the brush a hand blending oils,
> & colors a splatter across the table like de kooning
> – i watch this artist scoop artwork into her mouth.

SAMO AS AN ALTERNATIVE

— for jean-michel basquiat

~~i want to bask in basq~~
~~i want to bask in basq~~

i want to bask in psycho:
hastily woven be-bop basket
crafts sharp-line hue-slop funk;
hiero-prism heroism turned
heroin-ism quirked chroma-
pattern turned street prophet
zygote dropped drunk.

in this corner,
untitled black man versus.

exposé of said dead dread-head
exposes a pricked radiant smile
(dis)courtesy of same-ol' so-called
avant-garde samo was for.

bask in his haute height splattering
dabbing thru naught nights spattering
hanging with not-knights pattering
paint on frameless windows from which
he squints to see urban arcadia stripped
down to flesh and soul.

GUCCI SS17

alessandro michele's gucci of fantastical
whimsy and decadent nostalgia stages a
show resembling a venetian renaissance
fair in future ancient-china — his prints
like dead flowers: beautiful puffy gowns
in browns, mute greens, deep and dense
reds of blood & filthy wealth. machines
plume wispy white smoke like cigarettes.

nod to counterculture club kid deadbeat
eastern-western floral defunctive europe

models all pale and gawky in sheer satin
and thick suits appear from behind mist,
strut boudoir runway; mirrored sequins
hang above like chandeliers. music faint
and instead, strange as it seems, william
blake's *songs of innocence & experience* read
aloud, his words sinking into pink velvet.

nod to pop culture high brow streetstyle
denim chiffon golden dragon androgyny

RAF SIMONS SS02

we're still your *fear generation* – true then,
truer now how you prophesized to craft
poise from urban panic as if to suggest
we're our own enemy; *woe onto those who*

spit on the fear generation...
the wind will blow it back.

muslin headwraps mask grey faces;
long and sprawling garments drape
over tall slender bodies that sweep
barefoot; each march in red, carry
torch of youth to a doomed future
on sports courts in sport-coats motionless:

omen and manifesto?
searching for identity?
or fear of obscurity?

you in the background slouched
brazen, clean shaven, jeans cuffed
watching your destruction unfold

I INTERPERET

as if the sweeping drapes
when they fall her figure
punctuating the creases mean
more than i think: introduction
to my *needless to say*. i abandon soon

as she flicks posture no sooner than
what're you looking at? well art's what:

her accord between
form and fabric; her perpetual
untangling of webs; her woven
webs of which the seams seem
to speak volume.

i like to imagine my verse printed
on a raf simons coat that i would
work forever to afford her.

AFTERNOONS AT WINDOWS

and if you look
far
enough to see her
trash in my driveway you
will've looked past the vase
of asters resting
on the same sill where i lay
palms every morning peering out.

blotting sun.
quaffing brew.

breathing
smoke.

MARRIAGE

when two people are under the influence of the most violent,
most insane, most delusive, and most transient of passions,
they are required to swear that they will remain in that
excited, abnormal, and exhausting condition continuously
until death do them part.

— george bernard shaw

you and i fixed (daydreamingly)
like plastic ferns shooting glares
at the skin-crisping recumbence
of our distant eye: perchéd high
and golden, bound in stasis or vacuum
– counterpart to our twined bootstrings.

marriage is all-inclusive
it's selfish and altruistic it's
bathed in embalming fluid
it's vapid yet wholly mystic

tomorrow we'll gather nickels and
pick a piqué antique saffron dress
to address these pompous terrains;

maybe a blizzard picnic; or maybe
watch spectacular dusts flicker out
to shimmer madly in a hazy doze;
maybe feast on memories of cyclic
feasts on memories of now-ancient
devouring of venetian cobblestone.

but for now we can romanticize
the stench of old age and nameless fetuses.

WHO'S TRULY PLUCKING?

from ninth degree windows less blessed in
height than dementia i breathe algonquin,
its spelt gorges a scorchéd ornamentation
masked and sun-kist: *unfit lit cops can't censor*
my unfit sense of my once-unswarmed ornaments!

why've i lived life dry-puckered? to lip-kiss
mangled angel haberdasher stratospheres?
or to heedlessly feeble-wobble if provoked
cloaked in dystopia? thus a distrust latches
to synopses: *brolick chupacabra, dusty, broken.*

as merkel clinging strung dried in murking
dung lakes, i still instill high stilts instead
only to float unfolded instead only to load
strand-clipped, skin-colored cilantro leaves
into mouthports for undersourced diablos.

magnum opus: the orwellian bodega-clerk
picks old pixeld pics sold at farmersmarket
carpet-knitting juice tournaments circling
cashbag vintage-patterned rotunda clocks,
while cockcrowns cock back for monarchy.

no majesty! no magistrate! like an unmanned
manganese-smoke thrusting he(or)she(or)
hiroshima creole snacks wearily to where
we're heresy lapsed; i'm crushing crumble-
bee tins of undecadent lymphs wired shut.

who's truly plucking? she whose plucks'll
stop agelessness this agelessness this space-
lessness shifts twig fragments to godbodies.
step one's guns; and two's to smother ghee
slopped geese-roots upon mothertongues.

more flour they say, *flowers* they say, found it
lest that's my head my neck   i've let plop;
yet sock junk sweat's not bok choy clearly.
paleo-archetypal funguses grate meander-
sauce, for great neanderthal-steam craters.

look! a pork-shoulder mortician christening
sordid whence dipped in science-ion, heat
exiting miso through expired placebo lease.
ollie ollie oxen husk blotchless, of siberians
gaping one-eyed only in sundried sorcery.

send in the troops! troupes heave swinging fly-
sample masquerades with haggard placard
ferns towards their oppositional lens pores;
i am currently sitting in a box facing boxes
of spiked heart-wing amnesty-malted milk.

my ilk?   an elk soirée of ragheaded prisms
primmed for youthful truthlessness; sleuth-
posse lobbying for donald trunk's rutabaga,
mocking-up concave vortexes, and the like:
with corkscrew clouds as massive as el niño.

HYPERLOOP ONE

To consider only ways in which one might bleed and also be deterred is not only an insult but a mark of death— one I wear on my nape like peach-fuzz. Only then and with this knowledge can we reckon to recognize our recognizance before the eyes of God. I have since built my pyramid with Phoenix bones and, having carefully pulled plexiglass shards from out my calf, now walk in the path of Moses if Moses were to walk his path stutteringly in Parisian alleyways. I consider this lifetime no more than a blank slate. I consider my purpose with one eye on proverbs and the other pursuing rest. I consider a curated list of bad memories like: First, second, third, so forth.

An ultimatum: For every restless day I've stomached your hypothesis, I'm owed twice the earth's weight in precious spices. Then, in my grandmother's kitchen, we can finally flavor the lamb and feed our starving family. *Mise en place*, as it's called, is nothing more than a train of thought; and on this train, squirming in fabric seats that smell of old smoke, sitting slouchedly, passengers with dull fillet knives.

And on this train, the next stop is the first stop
but the last stop is near. But the last stop is near.

COUP D'ÉTAT

oh, cancerous vitriol!

i am *terrorist, sandnigger;* i am *raghead* lost
in search of self inside census bureau's
invisible box — i am *white?* not olive,

not tan, not scapegoat. but *white*
as page as privilege
as highway patrolmen.

oh, plagued tongue!

i am *colored, nigger,* methadone clinic;
menthol crystallizes my lungs.

i am *wetback, illegal;* a ghost
yet visible enough to plow.

i am
antithesis: *land of the free,*
home of the slave.

BIG SYRIA LITTLE SYRIA

the first syrians to this *new world* bring
turmeric roots & recipes pack on ships
with loud children women in colorful
headdress the men in ill-fitting trousers
reach ellis island & pack in tenements

the next syrians to this aging *new world*
barred from entering told to go home

as early as late 1800s those first syrians
from *sūriyya al-kubra*: damascus beirut
jerusalem aleppo leave the cedar trees
leave olive groves ancestral homeland
bring folklore & memories of fragrant
hibiscus trionum (or 'flower-of-the-hour')
they join the army they open bakeries
take family portraits on stoops & grow

recent as this morning syrian children
are piled high are plowed through the
bodies packed flesh to corroding flesh
washed up on european shores & left
in streets to rot the jets overhead drop
bombs not leaflets bombs not flowers
bombs where have the flowers gone?

ON DIASPORA

they said you'd be cracked or corpsed
left to prune in ancient brine.
they said: *young traveler,*
return to your neighbor who waits
to slip in your window
under your covers
into your mother
when you leave.

they said life's rotational: once a matter
of taste now a ration for life.

i pray you unsheathe, i said,
pray you digest the distance.

silence is like damascus.

ترجمة محمود درويش

mahmoud darwish:
selected translations by ahmad al-ashqar

from **Sparse Roses** (1984)

A DAMASCUS IN DAMASCUS

in damascus lies a damascus
for all times. friend for days
i've faulted you for resisting
my journey into a heartbeat.

is it not right upon my return
from love to question *why* you
leaned on daggers for me? or
why you lifted my ground only
to drop on me my own horse?

how i've wished to hoist you
toward a stream's beginning
or earth's end – *your beauty!*

& how beautiful damascus,
beautiful is she
– even with my wounds.

place half your heart in half
of mine friend to make one
large & righteous enough for
her, for me, for you.

for in damascus lies a damascus,
if you wish: a damascene mirror
for my soul.

IF I COULD REPEAT THE BEGINNING

if i could repeat the beginning
i would choose what i chose: a dog-rose

i would travel for a moment in the paths
that do lead and do not lead to cordoba

i would hang my shadow on two rocks
for homeless birds to build their nest
on my shadow's branches

i would break from my shadow
to follow the scent of almonds,
while it soars on a dusty cloud

i would tire at the slopes, say: *come*
listen to me / eat from my loaf / drink
from my wine / and don't abandon me
on the road of age like a tired willow

i love lands not breached
by a traveler's ode – lands
that don't abide by blood, or a woman

i love women who store in their desires
the suicide of horses on an edge

i would return if i could
to the same flower, the same step
– but i will not return to cordoba

AT THE BASE, ABOVE THE SEA, SLEEP

at the base, above the sea, above the cypress, sleep.
i have emptied for them a steel sky from memories.
doves flew in a direction determined by their claws,
east of their thoughts;   is it not their right to spray
upon the moon of water the wind of their names?

& if they plant in the trenches oranges,
                                        will it lessen gloom?

they sleep away from where the expanse tightens
above a base where words solidify; inside, rocks
anguished by phoenix bones. among us, a heart
that cannot approach *their* holiday of *their* things;
& among us,   a heart that cannot recover space
until these doves return to the earth's beginning.

            oh, you who sleep at the ends of earth:
            peace be upon you.

STILL IN THE PATH, A PATH

& still in the path, a path
still wide for the traveler.

we will throw many roses   into the river
to cut it. no widow wants to return to us.
we will go there,   go north of the neigh.

do you not forget that simple things birth
our future thoughts? speak on tomorrow
dear friend so i see my image in murmurs.

i will hold a dove's collar or find a flute
in a forgotten fig…yet my yearn whines
for anything;   its shot renders me killer
or killed.

& still in the path, a path to walk & walk.
but to where do these questions lead me?

i am from here & there yet neither here
nor there.   & i will throw many roses
before i finally reach my rose   in galilee.

THE GRAVE ROBBERS

will leave nothing to denote me for historians.
when weeds grow & my phantom escapes,

they sleep inside my corpse. they say what i do not
think; they forget what i remember; give my silence
their excuses. rest a bit, grave robbers, inside time
spacious enough for martyrs. there will be dialogue
about *time* with the killer, who is himself a martyr.

return to your families. maybe your children need
more to play with than my heart inside a shotgun
— need more than their surnames or brandnames
of clothing to walk to school.

do they not want to depart from
my old/new grave to elsewhere?

do they not want to identify a difference
between my golden shadow & a daffodil?

so who from among us is alive?
who is living in this play?

THE LAST TRAIN STOPPED

the last train stopped near the last sidewalk. no one
will rescue the roses. no dove will settle on a woman
due to words; time is up. the poem does not contain
more than butter does. don't trust our train oh love,
don't wait for people in traffic. the last train stopped

near the last sidewalk; no one wants to return to a
daffodil's reflection in mirrors of blackness. where
should i leave my final description for what a body
has done to me? what's ended has ended. where is
what ended? where can i unload what happened
to me because of *country*? don't trust our train, my
love. the last dove flew; the last train stopped near
the last sidewalk. & on it: no one.

I AM FROM THERE

i am from there possessing memories
born as all've been   i have a mother
a home with many windows   siblings
companions   a cell with a frigid pane

i have a tide now captured by seagulls

i have my own scene of lush pastures
the moon at my words' ends   great
bounty of birds   an eternal olive tree

on earth i have existed before swords
stiffened our bodies   i am from there
returning a weeping sky to its mother

i cry myself to be seen by impending
gloom   i have learned all the words
of bloody courtrooms   all the words
disassembled to reconstruct: *homeland*

MY ENTIRE AUTUMN

i search for myself, but the question sends me back–
nothing leads me to anything. space falls on gallows
& the field tucks   into the eye of a devoted needle.

i search for myself: *peace to those loved by sisyphus;*
peace to those illumined by my wounds. wind is for air
where my self is amongst a disturbance of itself, lifted
by marble & into dust.

this is my entire autumn,
higher than golden trees.
where do i go when i go?

in my lady's lap a place wide enough for two poems
& a planet's death.

all streets connect to the sky's corner without me.
so where do i go?

all streets expose them in deceptive whiteness
between beginning & end.   mother prepares
for me the morning on dishes of silver or oak.
i do not have my own mother,   only a mother
who waits there.

here a hand interrupts my days   & steals
what i prepare from words. words solidify,
a dove's ballad soars, & sleep itself sleeps.

but this anthem is not new to me,
nor the martyrs' commandments.
there is no beginning for the end;
no end for the beginning.

oh, trees: grow taller & taller! oh, trees: listen
so you can narrate broken like my first banners!
oh, trees: dazzle so that i see you in a grey dawn!

i explore for my self but the question sends me
back to a land without lands. land for the lands.

no, i cannot be what i was to them
whenever a cloud falls from a tree.
i searched for an earth to sustain…
& land for the lands.

no, i cannot be what i was to them
whenever i misplace a star. the path
to stars is lost as i am lost in myself.
where are those who were with me?
where is despair bursting between
two bodies? where are the prophets?

oh, trees: disappear within me
so i can mold my spirit from my own ruins!

oh, trees: break
so i can see my errors stretched within me!

oh, trees: explode so i can open
the window to my inner window.
my freedom & language explode.

peace to those loved by sisyphus;
peace to those illumined by my wounds.
peace to the wind.

from **Don't Apologize for What You've Done** (2003)

SAY WHAT YOU WANT

say what you want.   dot your letters.
place letters with letters to birth words
mysterious & clear, to produce speech.
place speech on a path; place the path
on a horse; place the horse on the pull
of someone distant; place the distant
with another distant… rhythm is born
when strange images interlock to join
the realist with the defiant surrealist.
have you written a poem? no!

perhaps: there's an excess or lack of salt
in characteristics. perhaps some accident
drained a shadow's symmetrical balance.
perhaps a vulture croaked in the highest
mountains. perhaps earth's just a symbol
muted in metaphor; thus it was annexed
by winds. perhaps it became too heavy
for the feathers of fiction. perhaps your
heart doesn't think well — so the poem
is tomorrow's bride, & the past his son,
housed in an obscure place
between writing & speech.
have you written a poem? no!

then,   what've you written?
i wrote a college lesson
& rejected poetry upon learning
the chemical makeup of a poem
…then i retired!

EARTH CONSTRICTS AROUND US

earth constricts around us trapping us
in the final hallway. we will yank out
our organs to pass. earth squeezes us.

if only we were its wheat so that
we could die & resurrect; if only
it were our mother to forgive us;
if only we were images of rocks
to be dreamt in our mirrored dreams.

we saw the faces of those
who will be slain in the final defense
for our spirit's ending. we cried
on their children's holidays. &
we saw the faces of those who will
throw our children from windows
in this final space; our stars buff
the mirrors.

where do we go after the final border?
where do birds fly past the final sky?
where do plants sleep after the final wind?

we will write our names with crimson vapor.
we will chop the ode's palm
so it's finished with our flesh.

here we will die. here in the final hallway.
here we will plant an olive tree with our blood.

I DO NOT KNOW YOUR NAME

i do not know your name.
name me what you wish.
you are not a gazelle.
not a steed.
not a dove in exile.
not a goddess.
who are you?
what's your name?

name me & i will be that.
i can't for i am wind,
estranged as you are &
each name has a land.
then i am 'no one'
but what's yours?

pick any name from the sky,
the one closest to 'oblivion'
& tonight i will be that.
i can't since i'm a woman
traveling on wind; you are
a traveler, too – each name
has its family & its home.

then, i am 'nothing.'

she corrected:
'no one.'
i'll fill your name with desire, my body
gathers you from every angle; my body
embraces you from every direction
until you become 'something'

& we will continue seeking life.

he said nothing. life is beautiful
with you, my virus.

NOTHING PLEASES ME

says a traveler on a bus. not the radio,
not newspapers, not the castles on top
of hills. i want to cry.

the driver says: wait until we reach the station
then cry alone as much as you'd like.

a lady says: me too. nothing
pleases me. i showed my son
my grave; he liked it & slept
without bidding me farewell.

an academic says: me too. nothing
pleases me. i studied archeology
without finding identity in rocks.
is this my truth?

& a soldier says: me too. nothing
pleases me. i am always trapping
the phantom that surrounds me.

the angry driver says: we are approaching
the last stop, get ready to get off...

so they shout: we need what's
after the last stop — so drive!

but i will say: drop me off here;
i am similar in that nothing pleases me,
but i am tired of traveling.

SLANTED ROAD

road that leads to egypt & damascus
(my heart rings from both sides)
road of the traveler from & into self
(my body a feather, space airy)
   of logic & mistakes
(i've made mistakes but tried)
   of ascent to heaven's terrace
(higher & higher, further)
   of descent to earth's threshold
(how grey the skies)
   of hopeful love
(that can turn wolves into busboys)
   of swallowing & the scent
   of oranges near the ocean
(the fragrance nostalgic)
   of spices, salt, wheat
(& of war, too)
   of peace, crowned in jerusalem
(after wars, a crusade against façades)
   of business & language,
   of dreamers
(all writing a noble story)
   of intruders' attempts
   to rewrite their history
(with a tomorrow consigned in banks)
   of conflicts in mythology
(in response   to technology)
   of abandoning, briefly, ideologies
(to advance worldliness)
   of panic over anything
(even angels fornicating)
   of agreeing about everything
(even a rock's gender)
   of the fascinating brotherhood
(between a carnivore & its prey)
road that leads to wrong or its opposite
(the surplus of similarities
between rhetoric & metaphor)

road of horses crazed by long distance
(& planes)
    of old recorded mail
(all letters stored in caesar's closets)
road that lengthens & shortens
(according to my father's mood;
he who is pleasant & prophetic)
road of goddesses with curved backs
(the flags of retreating armies)
    of a young lady who covers
    her privates with a butterfly
(the precious lapis stone
strips her of her clothes)
    of those perplexed by the description
    of an almond sliver
(its thickness translucent)
a long road without prophets
(they've already traveled the roughest roads)
road leading to the top
    of a home in shambles
(below a settlement's garden)

a road that forces another road,
until my phantom shouts at me:
    if you want to arrive
    at your turbulent self,
    don't tread clear paths.

THIS IS OBLIVION

this is oblivion around you: banners
that awaken the past, that press upon
remembrance. speedy time suppresses
traffic lights   & public spaces shutter.

oblivion is a marble statue — a statue
that fixates within you: *stand next to me*
to resemble me & place flowers on my foot.

oblivion is a repeating song — a song
that chases the housewife as a tribute
to happy occasions, into her bed, her
film room, her desolate   living room,
& her kitchen.

oblivion is monuments on the path
that take the shape of bronze trees
decorated with praise & falcons.

a cold museum void of tomorrow
that narrates the seasons selected
since the beginning of time. this
is oblivion: to remember the past
but not remember the story.

THE SHADOW

shadow is neither male nor female,
it is grey. & if within it i light a fire
it follows me, becomes larger, smaller.

i walk; it walked.
i sit; it sat.
i run; it ran.

i said, *i'll trick it by removing my blue coat*;
it followed, & set down its grey coat…
i turned onto a side street;
it turned onto a side street.
i said, *i'll trick it by escaping the sunset*,
but found it walking in front of me
in another city's sunset.
i said, *i'll return leaning on crutches;*
so it, too, returned on crutches.
i said, *i'll carry it on my shoulder*,
& it resisted.
so i said, *to trick it, i will follow it.*

i'll mock this parrot of shapes.
i'll copy that which copies me
so that the parallels align —
until i can't see it & it can't see me.

WEDNESDAY, FRIDAY, SATURDAY

wednesday, friday, saturday.
myth & *homeland* bear semblance.
if i had two hearts i would not regret love,
& if mistaken i'll say: i have hurt
my choices, injured the heart. the healthy
heart guides me to the springs.

thursday, lilies, monday.
the names of a place bear semblance.
in describing gloom i have exhausted
my song. the meaning sees the heart
of darkness, but it cannot see. words
have spoken words; many goddesses
cried over their roles.

judgement, sunday, tomorrow.
roads, tuesday, the sky bear semblance.
if i had two paths i'd choose the third.
exposed was the first path; exposed was
the last; exposed were the paths to the abyss.

THE CYPRESS BROKE

a cypress is a tree's sorrow, not the tree itself;
it has no shade of its own because it is the tree's shade.
— bassam hajjar

the cypress broke like a minaret & slept
in the road in its own austere shade, green
& dark as it is.   no one is afflicted by evil.
cars speed over its branches blowing
up dust on glass…the cypress broke
but the dove doesn't change its solemn nest
or its neighborly home.   two migrant birds
soar over its silhouette   trading symbols.

a woman asks her neighbor:
have you witnessed the storm? she replies:
no, nor a bulldozer…   the cypress broke.
those passing by say of the debris: perhaps
it broke from neglect or was aged by time,
for it's as tall as a giraffe with as much value
as a vacuum, unfit to shade lovers.
young boy boasts: i used to draw it
without mistakes, for its foundation is simple.
young girl cries: today the sky is incomplete
since the cypress broke. young man replies:
today the sky is complete *because* the cypress
broke. i say to myself: there is no ambiguity,
no clarity; the cypress broke, that is all
there is to say – that the cypress broke.

TWO OLIVE TREES

two ancient olive trees to the northeast:
in the first i hide to trick the storyteller;
in the other i hide poppy anemone
if i wish to forget…but i remember
i am filled with presence & select
my birthday to organize oblivion.

memories branch out. here is a moon
preparing a feast for absence. there,
a well in the south of the garden where
there is a wedding procession for a woman
& a devil.

all the angels i love
will take spring from here tomorrow
morning & grant me a volcano peak.
i am the second adam. i learned to read
& write from the lessons of mistakes,
& my tomorrow begins here. so now
if i wish to forget…i remember i chose
my beginning, born of my own accord:
not a hero, without sacrifice.

memories branch out & play. here
are two ancient olive trees, northeast:
in the first i found seeds of my song;
in the other i found a letter
from a roman commander:
oh, brothers of olives,
i ask your forgiveness,
i ask your forgiveness…

القسم الثاني

section 2

STAR OF BETHLEHEM

are the threads not our silken history?
its wool not sheep led by a shepherd
who speaks to them in the language
of coffee & sunflowers? or its detail
not millions of granules of dirt that
make up our brownish crimson soil?

        is it not woven in the way
        a ploughwoman furrows?

do you not produce threads from the land?
the red from pomegranate seeds the indigo
& hues of blue from *nilat sabbagh* the green
from sumac the black   from walnuts skins?

the eight-pointed star of bethlehem is named
for when the moon met a canaanite goddess.

are we anything
more than the fruit
of that exact moment?

______CIDE

tuck in to phosphorous
skies, cimmerian gaza;
& see sea's waves wade
contaminated mackerel
for the fishing.

shelter your blesseds
mama – lest your seeds
graze in seized / razed
trees' graves raking for
baba's uprooted vision.

broken mother channel
this mourning to detail
tales of fallen minarets
& stolen lineage singed
(unsung) as leaves burnt
from your family tree.

ode: to your olive tree,
your lemon tree – your
treeless farm.

owed: to their cast lead,
their iron dome – your
rayless sun.

or dayless son unlit like candles
paled in his empty room where
you weep parallel to idleness.

DÉGUSTATION

one dollop of green pea foam floats
over a single green tomato seasonal
& seasoned, its seeds shimmering to
reflect pulls, pools, droplets of demi
glace. in its shiny ceramic plate i see
my reflection at some farm upstate.

today's three course prix-fixe menu:
mesclun salad with feta, mint, lamb
one rack of lamb in blueberry glaze
& blueberry tart with crème fraîche

a scoop of hummus with the center
hollow absorbs olive oil, garlic, chili
& in its primitive bedouin pastiness
reflects the valleys, streams, screams
of my *teta*'s village in the west bank.

am i so lost in homeland-wanderlust
that i only see myself on *teta*'s porch?

am i a pompous dick to have taken
to work for lunch a tupperware of
truffled fois gras & french cheeses?

FLIGHT 1389

at turbulence the captain his voice
deep as cabin pressure announces
the closer we get to miami,
the smoother it should beget.

such odd diction for a pilot
who mans a domestic flight

where two toddlers cry: one real,
the other acting; armrest plastic
presses to knees; screens flash
advertisements, their lights
an orchestra bouncing through the cabin;
white man reads paper, brown man clicks
tablet, black man sits quiet; folks anchor
single-file near the restroom to pass time;
a slow, constant whir
rocks everyone to sleep.

the smell of cheap coffee-water
signals ginger ale soon, maybe chips.

MAN'S FATAL COLLAPSE

my first morning in east harlem
i walked through a cloud   thick
as bedouin pipe smoke (smelled
less of fruit, more of burnt tire)
& felt it scrape my heavy eyelids.

harlem and its
scents of   incense
            seafood
            sun-roasted piss

if pathmark across from dollar
slice is any indication of man's
fatal collapse, then a fall deep
as this is but parallel to a well;
but parallel   to a death;
but adjacent to a $1 slice:
poisonous and affordable.

harlem is as it's been for some time
a collection of buildings.   in them,

stories; in those, life. it's
brownstone and bullshit,
old school and plea. it's

get fly and stay fly, word up!

my eighth month i observe zombies
pressed chest-to-shoulder the naked
backs pressed up to a green scaffold.
an officer poses idly and grimaced,
minding everything but the scatter.

TO CHICAGO

— after carl sandburg

i regard the sandburg omen etched
in the wrinkly back of a pig's head-
rest, a (dis)*serve and* (un)*protect* memento:

> *they tell me you are crooked and i answer:*
> *yes, it is true i have seen the gunman kill*
> *and go free to kill again.*

we make tall industrial love intoxicated
in toxic spaces illumed by police lights;
sausage and pop burps both birth from
suited/zooted conductor speech ratlike
scuttling up steps piled in goliath's lips:
pilgrimage into the red line, blue line,
this is an orange line train
to midway.   doors closing.

remember downtown? pixelated faces
at the park spitting water on halfnaked
children? olden erections   mammoth
and modeling whorishly for plaid-clad
bearded slim dudes who (testing lenses
(and all's patience)) sway on the same
corners rum bums stumble past white
women and blackberry boys sprint past
desolate drifters?

i smoke in the elevator of our megalith
to dive into reddish-blue onyx of night,
swallowed whole.

TO BROOKLYN

i don't know you brooklyn

beyond a white pie at grimaldi's once
whence examining your yore
—now a trans-
forméd trans-
planted transience—in
the company of a nomadic alaskan,
i fretted entering recycle

as enemy.   not me.

fear of but not limited to:
flannel mustache   riding cappuccino uni-
cycle
past film noir screenings on dutchlande *slash*
warehouse *slash*
crackhouse *slash*
artspace.
and having spent recent wide-awakes
musing God & 3rd ave,
i find comfort fantasizing quaint mosques
draped brick-and-squalor

where young men shed
city grime like lightening bugs glint
neon-sign flickers before night
prayer, buzzing:
purge scraps from your streets
merge i into we
urge prospects to leave
befallen leaves in prospect.

because they
the reluctant, blanched
are your enemy. not me.

TO NEW YORK CITY

it was this moment   the bum murmurs &
lady sings herself loudly that i understand
new york city: polarity. it was this moment

leaving outside briskness & into platform
heat into train car   a/c beating our heads
that i finally understand alone & together
as one in the same.   & it's as we transport
through dimensions light   & dark back to
light on jampacked latenight subway   that
i make peace   with our decision to leave.

just one of millions of moments in which
i become a father, absorb debts, & escape
with one foot still buried in fresh dog shit.

OUTSIDE THE STATION

outside herald square station the cops
in packs of four or more patrol a park
now empty where black women men
white brown straight & queer upright
devout atheist & hopeless all marched
arms interlocked in unison in outrage

outside union square station   a group
hangs a silly trump piñata and charges
one dollar to take photo of or with it:
capitalism works in such a funny way

outside 125 & lex station poor people
go on   with their bodegas unchanged

THE TABLE

my wife jokes i care more about this table
than our son; so i respond *what's not to love*
about good design? she says something about
either family or finance, i can't remember;
i say a thing about food or propose a new

plan to spend more money.   she hates that

i spend all our money; i love how she thinks

wood and iron are comparable to humans –
flesh is one of the *rarest* material, of course!

we laugh about something
entirely   unrelated
                                        then go to sleep.

A SERIES OF SHORT ESSAYS

1. preamble

we the [disjointed] people
of the [un]united states; and so on.

2. helvetica

i once spent an entire semester
in an art class designing shapes
using only big helvetica letters;
the following semester,
i changed majors.

3. recycling

in new york one must promptly
discard waste into correct bins;
in syria one must try
to not be buried beneath it.

4. brevity

is a mother.

5. cannibalism

to eat another's flesh your teeth
sinking into soft back meat
is truly bizarre, unless for ritual
or if you *have to.*

CANNIBALISM

under streams of thick pixelated waves and grave
pretensions i've indeed
dived in infinite seas
of to be

eaten from within;
beaten to a pulp

and risen from blight like
slithery python to implant
remorse in my blood;
therefore into yours.

while exhaled winds of flutes
hoot cacophonous atop roof-
tops where sous chefs chop
bleu-greens over two sides of
lukewarmish bourgeois soup,

i light local cigars toast
empty cups for her coup

lest youth's acid resumes traffic
consumes passages secretes
rumi lines onto cracked leather
of not-roomy coop. *coupé,* says

she who undresses me
in a corridor un-veiling
me to my truth: i've lost
myself in finding you.

TOOK IN

the printed mention of his name
a pleasure so he   paused

for a sunrisen moment,   feeling.
eyes'd been refreshed by the sight.

> *but i've a comrade   who's on his*
> *way to catch the noon train under*
> *loads of bags and dressing cases.*

a settled look of dullness began early
september, and he was returning; *he*,
an old word for bachelor,   isn't it?

this moment smiling back he wished
he knew –   wished he
could retreat to enjoy   the sensation
as often as possible.   how delicious

to have a place like this.

A BEGINNING & AN END

an unending tree   an unending tree
upended has left earth clefts where soil
lives i am roots father of root particles
and megalithic punctures — if for this
reason my skin cracks   i will have died
justly but while i've yet to pass the look
of vibrating cheek fat & trembling eyes
is nearly enough to crush me: such as

with that one look in one's eyes where
suns rise & nights fall a clumsy wobble.

my summer? mad / sweaty / tyrannical.
a wedding, which is to say the beginning,
& the beginning of the end of another's.

we woke our son from sleep still
in his sleep-sack to voices – both
weeping & growling – to escape
what at the time felt a nightmare.

we made our way down highways
lit only by a sequence of red eyes
in the back of semi-trucks staring
us down like his (deep bloodshot)
when he broke me,   his wrinkled
cheeks pulsing before we packed.

we paused in hudson the next day
to admire buildings; we ate cheese
for dinner, drove home in silence.

AM INTERNET

in purest form   am gadgetry & tech-
no-logical scrolls down informations
down rabbit holes   down downloads
of intelligence & bullshit bandwidths
wide as bull torso am a surfed ocean
sensory   deprivation of information
overload/ downunder upload speeds
of light which when intensified blind
case study control group insomniacs
am viral viral viral malware virus spy

though i am also: apocalypse farmer
i pick cracked weeds weeds — a seed
lacks energy/ lax synergy/ lags at its
slapdash roots & its roots command
like command line root to command
sudo/ pseudo-access to its shiny core

[DARKORCHID INHALING]

— in the spirit of roberto harrison

i won't
i repel —

i pierce the invasion of gravity's drag
indulge in the sorrow of yesterday's smiles
retreat to an angle and sink through my guts

i indent
i observe and implode
i deserve to unsheathe

i surrender my ground to unbearable warmth
drown in the snow of the trojans within
meet apprehension with buckets of God
i kneel

i am hope in the trash
skeptical math
imperfect flowers
and radius length

i gather the excess and hollow the graves

NOT A SELF PORTRAIT

i do not come from bedouins was not
born in a moist desert have not spent
28 years trying to explain myself not
eager to please others   i never think
of others i only ever consider myself

i do not care for structures and boxes
completely opposed to structures am
deeply opposed to boxes i shudder at
thoughts of form i find something to
be desired in gardens   and repetition
something to be desired in television
and fashion the architecture of rome

i am not obsessive or compulsive not
easily sold on items nor hasty making
decisions not willing to pause & think
of consequences of actions   if faced
with any resistance   i cannot counter
with friction free from illness & pain

i am not a son and not a father   not
a husband or a lover not an uncle or
a brother nor subject to *random search*

A VALID COMMENTARY ON TIME & SPACE

The problem with *time* & with *space* is mathematical: One of pluses, minuses, angles, blackboards. How then in our literary numberlessness do we approach this?

HEAD-ON WITH
HARDS-ON, OR
TREPIDATION?...

Here's how: Earth skin: Soft when pressed. Soft as razor blade gash across cheek flesh, yet hard as a friend's lie. How much less vital to our understanding of egg (yolks, nog, etcetera) is our understanding of water?

Brought to mind are fragrant memories of parks, black with life, fermented.
Another, of simplicity. There's often too much to say about minimalism.

But who are we to change the essence of Roma? God? In this I relive a 1960s I've never smelled atop a cliff overlooking beige valleys of wild grain; mid-city they're slaughtering goats, I suppose.

I've a shirt to prove this, blood still in it, two-sizes too-small.

O, the kingly green of Bohemia!
O, dead syntax of my Ancients!

The cliff crumbles; gravity trails it. The villagers mad as fish-grease pick fallen limestone chunks from the valley & sling them towards the clouds. The cliff is reborn, this time

a mountain.

I regard horizons as young sparrows do tree-trunk vastness, with intrigue; & weigh consequence like my elders do, with tourniquets.

In dreams I'm pious; awake, deadly.

But what of ...SPACE?

Most days I regret not having accidentally tried peyote. Such & such is fatherhood. Now a marksmen I've less leeway. Kindred competes with my longing for figs & olives, the trees whence they blossom & are plucked, the loud scent of my soily homeland.

Home is the stiffest mystery. In the last hour I've'd three, while having none.

Most days I'm particles in the valley breeze wafting
between Mount Curse & Mount Blessing; all other
days I'm my mother's favorite headscarf draping,
its frilly edges clutching her warm chest as I'd once.

AHMAD AL-ASHQAR is a nomadic, romantic, obsessive Palestinian-American poet, translator, and educator. He was born in Kuwait, but soon after his birth, at the start of the Gulf War, his family was displaced first to Jordan and then to the United States. He spent much of his life in Chicago, where he remained close to his traditions and roots in a large, thriving Palestinian community. Ahmad first fell in love with language through rap music and spoken word, before discovering his love for written poetry. After graduating from the University of Illinois at Chicago, he moved to Dubai to teach English at the high school level, before returning to the U.S. to complete an MFA in Creative Writing at the New School. He now lives, writes, and teaches in Dubai.

MAHMOUD DARWISH (1941-2008) was regarded as the Palestinian national poet. He published more than 30 volumes of poetry, won numerous awards for his works, and was translated into 20 languages. As a young man living in Haifa, Darwish faced house arrest and imprisonment for his political activism and for publicly reading his poetry. After joining the Communist Party of Israel, he left for Russia, where he attended the University of Moscow for one year, and then moved to Cairo. He lived in exile for twenty-six years, between Beirut and Paris, until his return to Israel in 1996, after which he settled in Ramallah in the West Bank. He died in Houston, after complications from heart surgery.

Printed in Great Britain
by Amazon